Trademarked Under The Invisible Backpack™

Tribute

To ALL who have lost a loved one to Suicide.
A special Tribute to a man who has saved my life on three occasions by his own death!
The Late Great Robin Williams

The Invisible Backpack Team the Real Courageous One's

Word Smith - Vera Currie
The Amazing One - gina Van Wormer
My Listening Ears - Deb Stover
Agent - Sherrie Johnston
The Wise One -Connie McDonald
Graphic by Terry's Embroidery — Mykaela McGrew Higgins
The Brave Ones
    Bill and RoLane Hartwick
    Hilary Fahning
    Mike Mouldon
    Sean Smith
    My Crescent City Dutch Bros Kids
    Sharon Frymer
    Black Trumpet
    Lisa Borath
    Darin and Marcy Bradbury
    Paige Swan
    Donna Zorn

The Cowans
My Bookings Divas
Louise Fugate

## Table of Contents

Thanks for Being Honest
Don't Misunderstand Me
Live and Learn
The Choice is Yours
One Giant Step
Regret
A Degree
I Offer You
Give and Return
Sense of Accomplishment
Tonight
Heart Strings
Patiently I Wait
Joint Effort
I'm Honored
Inundated
Perseverance
Mistakes
Please Stop
Tenderness
I Have A Dream
Life's Many Treasures
Fragile Heart
Nature Walk
It Will Happen
Let it Out
Clearing The Clouds
Christmas
Piano Man

Dear Friend
It is All Mine
I Like
The Game
Feelings
The End Results
Kids
Marathon
Tre Boys
Season Finale
A Poem is
If I Could
There is a Time
Grading
Soon
School
Beginning of The End
No Title
Someone
The Class of 2000
Best of The Best
Worthwhile
Two Way Street
No Title
So Long
Finally Over
Mask
Morgan
Mrs. Daniels

Christmas
Participating
Frustrated
True Love
Liar
Tourette's

January 8, 1992

This mother loves you with
all of her heart!
    What joy I find in a son
so caring and smart.
    Live life to its fullest in all
that you do.
    Keep Gods word and the
Golden Rule.
    When times are rough as
they often are
    Rise above and reach for
the star.
    Strive for your goals
in all that you do.
    Remember money is useful,
but only a tool
    It can make you prosper
or make you the fool.
    Be true to yourself and
those that you love
    "Enjoy, Life", Gods greatest
gift from above.
        Love always,
            Your bestest Mom

William L. Hartwick

1080 E Lassen AVE #43

Chico, CA 95926
(916) 891-3340
$100°° Reward if returned

Date

Jan 2nd 1992

" Reality
What
a
Concert "

# FORWARD

YOU ARRIVED IN OUR FAMILY AT QUITE AN EARLY AGE AT FIRST YOU DIDN'T TALK MUCH, A VERY SHORT LIVED STAGE YOU GREW UP TAGGED DUPPY BY FRIEND THELMA LOU A SILLY LITTLE NICKNAME THAT STAYED A PART OF YOU THERE ARE MANY NUMEROUS THINGS THAT I RECALL HOWEVER • ACCIDENTS • STAND OUT ABOVE THEM ALL WHATEVER THE TASK YOU WERE ALWAYS SURE YOU COULD WIN AND IF YOU DIDN'T YOU SIMPLY TRIED AGAIN YOU HAVE A GENTLE SPIRIT AND A VERY ACTIVE MIND THE TEACHERS WERE AMAZED HOW YOU CONNED THE KIDS IN LINE YOUR GREAT REPORT WITH CHILDREN AND YOUR ELDERS TOO THIS IS AN ATTRIBUTE THAT IS REALLY YOU SPORTS YOU LOVED, MATH YOU EXCELLED STANDING UP FOR WHAT IS RIGHT NEARLY GOT YOU EXPELLED ON TO COLLEGE TO JOIN THE ELITE GET A DEGREE AND JOB...MAKE LIFE COMPLETE IT SEEMS JUST LIKE YESTERDAY THAT YOU WERE SO SMALL AND NOW YOUR A YOUNG MAN GROWN HANDSOME AND TA LL BE THANKFUL FOR EACH DAY, EACH MOMENT AND EACH YEAR THIS IS A GIFT DENIED MANY I FEAR YOUR LIFE'S JUST BEGINNING ON THIS DAY OF YOUR BIRTH BREATH IN ITS BEAUTY AND CHALLENGE THE EARTH
WRITTEN BY ROLANE HARTWICK

# Trauma

It happened at birth a coma for me, for others I'm not sure
The fact of the matter is, there is not cure
It comes in many avenues from physical to the mind
There is no defining it, no particular kind
Some have it for a lifetime, some right away
If we don't deal with, forever will it stay
Exposure to so many has really made me ache
Accepting my own trauma has really made me wake
The pain is deeper than I ever thought it could be
As I open my heart to others they can clearly see
How much I am hurting over this recent tragic loss
Not only losing my wife but dealing with a horrible boss
What I am realizing is that I am not alone
Coming together with complete strangers and seeing how they have grown
Gives me inspiration way beyond belief
Never did I imagine there could be so much relief
I thought I was alone suffering this awful pain
Thinking I was crazy, literally going insane
Listening to their stories as they share their lives with me
Has surely made realize I can plainly see
That trauma is a creature that comes in many ways
I am thankful for this experience and cherish all my days
As I wake each morning wondering what the day will bring
And listen to birds outside my window sing
I can't help but think and hope that each day brings a smile
To everyone's lives that's here on earth for only a little while
I pray to God each night as I lay my head down to rest
That ALL our trauma lives will turn out for the best
My trauma is forever, but my heart is now stronger
For human bond and love of life will last even longer

By
William Lane Hartwick
July 13, 2018
Life Healing Center

# Bailey and Justin

I know you are wondering what you can do
And why I went away
Somehow life got away and this is what I say
My career as a principal was ended for no reason they will
tell
I didn't handle that very well, it's been a living hell
I came to the Life Healing Center seeking help to retool
my life
After all I got so bad I even lost my wife
But most of all you two are it the ones I love the most
I am healing very well soon to return to the coast
Each day that goes by my heart opens and my life is
coming back to me
I'm coming home to be your dad and you'll soon see
I love you both more than you will know
Can't wait to hold you tight
Until that day comes may you rest a peaceful night

# Teaching

So you want to be a teacher
Educate the leaders take
Someone has to take on that responsibility
How can you expect our kids to
Survive on their own
If to them, our knowledge, we never
Ever loan
It is not an easy task
The one mentioned above
It all starts in the home with a concept
Called love
You could have a bachelor of science and
A master's in fine art
But it takes a doctorate in life
To set great teachers apart
Unless you are willing to learn
From those who already know
You've put limitations on yourself
Never allowing you to grow

For teaching is not always in a classroom
At school
It is the sharing of lives
Experiences that is a valuable tool
I have made the choice to commit my
Life to teach
In every child that needs my love
Out to them I do reach
If you have made the same decision
In your mind and in your heart
Give those kids a fighting chance
By offering them a head start

# Children are so Precious

How can anyone get so mad they must abuse a child
They have so much joy to give you in a manner that is
so mild
They are so honest in the way that they speak and how
they judge us all
Don't abuse that child's morale let them stand up tall
Remember what it is like to crawl before you could walk
Please don't strike that child sit down and have a talk
Show them what is to like and believe in a spirit
Don't show them pain and agony let them feel you're
hurt
Turn it over to your God let those feelings of anger be
stripped away
Enjoy your relationship please don't lead them astray
Please remember words you speak can never be taken
back
So before you tongue lash a child think of the damage
retract

# Life's A Gamble

Pick up a dart and give it a throw
where it lands is where you go
Making a decision right now is hard
Take a deck, pick a card
Take a chance on red or black
Turn your head and don't look back
Draw five cards and in your hand you will hold
Don't ever think about it, don't ever fold
Just pull that handle and pull it again
Sooner or later you will win
That pot of gold Life does show
It is years to have, it's time to go

# Climbing That Mountain

Life is too short to get upset and mad
Just hold up your chin and be glad
That you are healthy and able to be
Whatever your mind's eye can see
Go for the gold and settle for nothing less
Be all you can be, be the best.
With the qualities you possess, and ability to do
Not even this cruel world can stop you
Grit your teeth and lower your shoulders
Throw out your chest and be much bolder
Get it together and reach for the top
Whatever you do, just don't stop

# DiNero♡

It is green, rectangular, and a pain in the butt
Recently it has put me in a rut
Dig my way out is what I will do
All I need is a little help from you
To guide me straight on how to play
But before I do, make sure I can pay
For this money when I get in the hole
Sometimes I think I am a bank roll
But now I know this is not true
For helping me realize, I say thank you.

# Cognition

Knowledge is a word used everyday
Just find a way to use it, just find a way
To grab all you can and shallow it down
Make sure you digest it through and sound
Life's best gift is that of the mind
It is out there, it's yours to find


# Inquiry

No matter where we go, no matter what we do
Life always has questions for you
What to buy, where to go, what is your opinion
what is your choice.
Someone somewhere wants to hear your voice
So crawl under a rock or busy your head
Hold your opinion until you turn red
Sooner or later yours will appear
Let it out for all to hear

# Growing

What is up and what is down
My head seems to be spinning around
I want to be settled down and on my way
To make my future each and every day
I guess fear plays a big role
In whom I am and where I go
One day at a time is how I should be
But that is really hard for me
I need to bear down and swallow my pride
From you I ask a hand in guide
Where to go, what to do
That is the question I am asking you

# Road to Success

When opportunity knocks open the door
To expose yourself to all the more
Take a look both hard and long
Decide for yourself what is right or wrong
Then make a commitment that you do choose
Just stick to it, you cannot lose
With the attitude to succeed and willingness to change
Your entire life can rearrange
You will get what you want, want what you see
And live the rest of your life very happily

## Just Because

♡n a day as special as this
Pucker up for a great big kiss
As ♡ur lips touch a twang is felt
Somewhere down below my belt
My heart beats fast as a r♡aring train
Rushing bl♡♡d up t♡ my brain
S♡ let's sit down with a glass ♡f wine
H♡ney will y♡u be my valentine

# Time

It comes and goes and doesn't stand still
Take advantage of it all you will
One day you have plenty, the next it is gone
It moves fast from night to dawn
So look around you and hold on tight
Before you know it's the very next night
Experience each tick the best you know how
For time is yours, the time is now

## Decisions

I hate to make them for how they make me feel
But if you don't make them, someone will
It is your prerogative to make your own
It's up to you and you alone
We don't always make the right one
But we make them so they are done
Every day of our lives, they are here
Decisions to make, the next one is near

## Awakening

As the sun streaks thru the crack in the curtain, I
awaken with a smile, I lean over and see you sleeping
ever so happily
With a smile so wide, I press my lips
Ever so softly against your cheek,
And you awaken
I smile, you smile and another beautiful day in our lives
together has begun

## Mom and Dad

I get jealous because I lack self-confidence
It is not bad to lack, but I need to build
I ask that you work through this with me because I do
not know anyone I would rather have help me than you

# Proposal

As the days go by, my love for you grows
I had to write to let you know
My heart is yours for the rest of my days
I know I have yours in so many ways
I think of marrying you every moment of my life
That one day seeing you will be my wife
You are warm and make me feel so loved
That's why I put you on a pedestal that rises above
Your left hand is naked and awaits for thee
I can't wait for the day you marry me

# Promises

I am not promising our lives together will be easy
I am not promising you we will be wealthy
I am not promising you we will not have differences of opinion
I am not promising you I will be perfect
I am promising you I will love you, listen to you, respect you, and give you a life filled with joy
I am promising I will work through with you Whatever obstacles we encounter
I am promising you I will support you in whatever you do
And most of all I am promising I will let you live your life however you want even if it disagrees with me
Why do I make all these promises, because of promise number one, I love you

## JFK

In his mind's eye, he tried to do what was right
Influential people around him put up a fight
The end result was an undeserved death
How it happened is still a myth
For these people to cover up is such a shame
To one man they pointed the blame
Beneath all the wrong the truth does lie
Somewhere in the influential eye


## RFK

Then he came along to back
Up his thoughts
Just like his brother, he got shot
Once again, his death goes
Unknown
Blamed on one, one alone
This all seems like fiction
It can't really be
People killed, fighting for you a me
How is it that we let them
Get away with murder
Never letting it be locked into any
Further

# I'm ♡K You're ♡K

Everyone is dealt a different deck of cards
Making life easy or making life hard
Take what you get without fear of guilt
Then turn around and look at what you have built
By using knowledge, pride and wit
You'll get what you want, just don't quit.

# Myself

Sometimes I say things I don't mean
Not always that witty, sometimes not that keen
I like to apply humor to all that I do
Making each day exciting and new
When I am happy, I share it with all
Makes others feel more proud and stand more tall
Giving a pat on the back and a cheery little grin
Makes for a more positive environment for all to be in
So, no matter when, no matter where
Keep your sense of humor and you will prosper

# Team Work

Looking ahead at the year to come
There will be people that make it, there will be some
We all have goals that we want to come true
It will happen for me and you
By pulling together and working as one
We can do it, we can get it done
Just remember thru thick and thin
It takes a group effort for us to win
So when times get tough, remember to smile
It helps us all go that extra mile

# Me

As the years go by our lives do change
Mine has recently rearranged
I have taken a step that has opened my mind
The life I have been looking for, I will soon find.
I am my own person that I do know
This individual has awaken and is ready to grow
To experience this life that I do choose
No matter what happens I cannot lose
Because I am doing what is best for me
I am living for today very happily and free

## The Great ♡nes

Wh♡se words these are I think I know
Tw♡ gentlemen by the name ♡f Edgar Allen P♡e
Have been influential in the words I write
Giving me the ability t♡ use my insight
F♡r poetry when written is h♡wever y♡u feel
T♡ me it is th♡ughts that are extremely real
The ab♡ve menti♡ned men have d♡ne it s♡ well
I want my th♡ughts t♡ be kn♡wn f♡r all t♡ tell
S♡ when th♡se words feel up with sn♡w
And we are enlighted again by Mr. P♡e
Just remember p♡etry is whatever y♡u want
N♡ matter what subject, n♡ matter what f♡nt

# Point St. George

Its surface can be rough or as calm as sleep
The life it supports runs ever so deep
As the waves crash hard against the rocks
The boats stay nestled close to their docks
The brave try to challenge this powerful source
Some of them winning, some losing, of course
To be out on her is a trill of its own
Or just to watch her work while you are alone
The ocean's beauty does so much for me
Watching the boats fight that treacherous sea

Dedicated to
Thomas Lee de'Arth

# Think About It

These are many things that force us to change our
ways
Some may take a lifetime, some only a day
But now we are faced with a much harder choice
Go ahead, open up, and let them hear your voice
For lives are being risked for what, a little fun
When actually they could be saved with more education
Aids is not funny, it is a serious ordeal
Just open your eyes and see it is for real
The next time you decide to have a little fun
Remember, it could be your last, this could be the one

# Friends

This is someone you always stand by
No matter what, no matter why
Someone to confide in, someone to love
Someone that always rises above
Listens to you cry, watches you smile
Sticks with you for that very last mile
A person you care about day in and day out
A friend is a friend, without a doubt

# Be True

You try to be honest, fair and sincere
Most of the time people don't care
They look at you like you can't be true
You have to be lying to do the things
you'll say that you'll do
This is ok, because truth lies within
the eyes of the beholder and
that of a friend
Continue to be honest and live
Without shame
And those around you will soon do the same

.

# Starting Over

Life is too short to sit around and wait
It is time to go out on that very first date
Explore this moment like untouched land
At the least you will have is a new friend
Don't worry about the past and enjoy the night
Who's to say what is wrong or right
It could wind up as a joyous event
Or perhaps, maybe, you shouldn't have went

## Parachuting

Falling from the sky at an unbelievable speed
Being assisted mentally by a previous feed
The feeling of freedom, an ability to fly
Exploring all avenues of the great blue sky
Then peaceful as heaven and quiet as sleep
You float down with a moment to keep
For now life is a much great place
Being able to understand this human race

# Expressions

It is hard for me to tell people how
I feel
Letting others down is a fear that
Is real
I always think through all the ins and outs
Then present my opinion without a doubt
If people do not like it, I guess that's
Too bad
I have to live for myself and what make
me glad
To go on each day, one expression at a time
Not always through needs, but perhaps as a mime

## Sunset, Sunrise

As the sun sets on another beautiful day
I am glad to have experienced it in so
many ways
Spending time with family, friends and foe
Is always a joy no matter where you go
For these are the people that make
life neat
Being with them each day is a special treat
As the darkness settles in and the
days end is near
I look forward to tomorrow
without any fear
With people in my life as special as this
I can't wait for the sun to wake me with her kiss

# Death and Dying

I do not understand the concept of dying
People have explained it or at least they are trying
Some do not make it to that day of birth
Others last forever on this earth
Who's to say it is your time to go
I find it upsetting that I will never know
So live each moment the best you know how
For today is tomorrow, today is now

# The Devil's Dandruff

There is nothing good about them
No matter how you look
Some people pull through them
Some turn into a crook
Avoid them at all cost
For those who use them end up lost,
In a world that my look good
But is really wrong
Some stay for a short while, others quite long
Best bet is to never get involved with drugs
You will find something works better like giving hugs

# Free bird

With each new experience comes a new day
Like watching the wind choose its way
By overcoming obstacles with an intelligent thought
Allowing the mind to work not letting it rot
Take that freedom and put it to good use
Live how you want, I choose to live loose
Don't abuse what you have at hand
Make it like music and you are the band

# Today

How things change ever so fast
Some moments come and go, some really last
One day it seems like it is about to fall
Then from a distance you hear a call
Of great magnitude and timing so right
You can feel the gravity, it is in sight
Enjoy the moment but move ahead with pride
Find the next victim that dare does hide

# How I Write

I like creating the things I do
Like writing these thoughts for me and you
I have a certain style of displaying a thought
It makes me feel good to share a lot
I then look over each and every word
To make sure it does not sound too absurd
I make the changes that seal the deal
And what you have is a feeling this real

# Relationships

Isn't it strange how we get through each day
Causing our own pain along the way
Shouldn't we be happy with just our own self
Letting only those share with us who deserve the
wealth
It makes sense to me to enjoy my life each day
Not allowing anyone to get in my way
On the same note caring for others, not causing any
hurt
Don't mess with others feelings, don't even flirt
Just be honest, up front and sincere
And if the energy is wrong, don't let them get near

# Mrs. Right

We meet new people everywhere we go
Very few do we ever get to know
You, on the other hand, I have known for awhile
When I think of you, I can't help but smile
It is time to take that curiosity and see
If I am right for you and you for me
I know it takes time, but we have waited quite long
I know in my heart it is right, it can't go wrong
For we are finally at the point of no return
Destiny has its course, it just took a while to learn

# Reunion

Your smile is that of a moonlit night

Making everyone around you feel so bright

Seeing you again made my heart race fast

Reminding me of a wonderful past

From age five, to your beauty today

I have thought about you, all the way

Seeing you again gives me feelings of

Your spirit about you makes me feel like a little boy

So don't lose your smile, you deserve the best

Kim, you are a beautiful person, more so than the rest

# Fond of You

The time we spent together made my heart grow near
It showed me how special you really are, my dear
All these years I really did know
I cared for you and admired you so
You have these qualities most people strive for
Your spirit and love I would like to share more
Patience is a virtue that I need to learn
I will wait forever to experience my turn
All the others did not realize what they had
That is good for me, but for them, too bad
Because even if we never end up as one
You're in my heart from dark till sun

## You and Me

Cupid and his arrow live for today
Making sure love finds its way
Into your heart fling shall be shot
Hoping it hits that very special spot
Since in my quiver only one arrow does stand
I have picked your heart for it to land
For you have won my heart and now I shall see
If you feel the same way about me
You are so lovely, beautiful, and kind
Will you be my Valentine

# Go For It

It is time to move on and follow that light
That seems to touch me late at night
Pulling me away from my current place in time
Leading me towards that new birth of sunshine
For in my heart I need to carry on
I've learned pleasing myself is really not wrong
Home is where I feel the most like myself
Not being there seems like I'm dust on a shelf
Take the actions necessary to pull ahead real soon
Be where you want by the very next moon

# Come and Gone

One person's ego is another's downfall
Don't let it affect you, just stand up tall
Go for what you believe in and what you think is best
Grab a hold of what you want and throw away the rest
Everyone offers their opinion to you
Decide which ones you chose to listen to
After all is said and done and your mind is clear
That egotistical person somehow does disappear

# Missing You

I would travel through rain to see you smile
Tread through snow that extra
Knowing you're there waiting for me
Makes my heart beat endlessly
Outside its storming, new snow is born
Inside I think of you keeping my heart warm
With each tick of the clock, our meeting grows near
But for now in my mind your presents is here

## Mt. Shasta

Her magnitude and ambiance stand clear on earth
Displaying enormous, strength and girth
Dormant for now yet capable of awakening
Her beauty is magnificent, simply breathtaking
To her peak I soon will journey on
Knowing she will allow me to see far beyond
Each moment I have in the presence of this creation
Is time spent with God's gift to salutation
A visual phenomenon that few will ever see
Use your imagination and visualize it thru me
Her snowcapped tips are a year round sight
As they glisten with beauty from the bright moonlight

# Eye

I had an experience the other day that engaged me to write this
down
Home is where I want to be in that little town
But first you need to learn the other side of we
Twisted and turned upside down, this is the real me
First and foremost my current career is out
I'll sacrifice whatever it takes to make it without a doubt
Now for what inspires my soul
what I really want to do
This is where there is a difference between me and you
I want to be an educator for the young to learn
I feel I have a lot to offer and I am a bit concerned
Kids these days feel a lot of animosity
Drugs, sex and alcohol are a problem you see
I'm not just interested in teaching them how to write
I want to show them individualism and how hard they must fight
To be whatever they want no matter what that may be
As long as it is healthy and it allows them to be free
I also want to act to let my emotions out
There are so many characters inside me
I need to scream and shout
Up front, at first, I am a funny guy
I am now open and honest, in the past I had to lie
The drugs are gone and my emotions stand tall

For portraying all these characters is seeming a ball
I guess I really am an actor, just to have a very few
I now want to share my thoughts with people like you
On the big screen or live at Carnegie Hall
This is where I need to be; I can hear my beckoning call
As I age and understand who I am
One of my characters inside me has become my biggest fan
There are so many people that have a special place in my life
It is time to settle down, start a family with a wife.
My mother is #1. I love her for all she is worth.
Combined with my father, they're the best parents on earth.
That male figure lead I mentioned briefly above.
He's become my best friend and someone I really love.
My brother and I are quite opposite yet in the same mind.
I have a lot to offer him one day, he will soon find.
I am concerned about his health, due to all the stress
He needs to stop and smell the roses and take a little rest.
Gayle is a quite a woman and I love her a lot.
Recently we have become close, who would have ever thought
The wife, the family and soon even a child
The "Kid" as a father, now that sounds wild
As I look ahead and see myself grow
I am headed in the right direction, this I do know.
It feels real healthy to finally be free.
Thanks for taking your time to get to know me.

# The Shot

That experience I had.  It happened again.
With extremely bright lights and cameramen
On center stage with freedom to be
Whatever anyone wanted to make of me
I feel the best shots are the ones I design
By seeing it previously happening inside my own mind
At first, the results were quite a let down
But the more I looked, there is something I found
By studying my work, listening, and learning from all
This acting stuff is going to be a ball.

# It's My Own Fault

I went against my intuition and relied on another
Even if it is your best friend who is just like a brother
You have no control of all the obstacles we overcome
For when others fail you, you feel real dumb
If you would have planned ahead for all human error
You would not be holding a handful of your own hair
As sure as the sun rises and sets each day
We are responsible for ourselves along the way
So take on the challenge without any fear
For you can't escape what you see in the mirror

♡, Sherrie

I left when you did, but I could not stay away
I have never had an experience quite like today
Handed an envelope filled with such joy
My eyes teared up as if I were a little boy
For at that moment I knew for sure
I will be a teacher because of people like her
The kids I took to, like they were my own
Enjoying each moment we had along
Their little smiles and bright little cheeks
Will be easy to see for forty some weeks
I hope one day to give it all back
Thanks for sharing interest where others did lack.

# Home Sweet Home

The freedom to think and mind to see
What is really happening to me
Growing by the minute in leaps and bounds
That life I was looking for, I just found
My instincts were right, to home I journey on
That mountain top let me see far beyond
To experience a taste of what I want to be
Was enough reassurance to agree with me
For I made the decision that I did fear
Home Sweet Home I am finally here

# Love of All Kinds

Some seem to be only temporary, like at first sight
Others may go well into the night
It could be feelings that are romantic, you see
Or simply someone who really cares about me
Possibly a friendship that runs real deep
Or perhaps a moment that you will always keep
Doesn't necessarily have to be between
Woman and man
It could be for sporting team and you are a fan
It is often displayed for God up above
Don't deprive yourself, learn how to love
Before you share with others, make sure you know
your own
For love is nothing if you are alone

# The Walk

Their little minds are hard at work
Noticing the horse stuck in the murk
What is living, what is not
Making a decision via a thought
From trees to cars, mountains and signs
Observing the expansion of their minds
Their camaraderie runs through them all
Their smiles indicate they're having a ball
After all is said and done, we have returned
A new experience for all and one in which we learned

## Del Norte County

This earth we live on is such a beautiful place
It is indicated by the smile on your face
From the tip of a redwood tree at the highest
mountain top
Or where the river meets the ocean, life doesn't stop
The air up here is as pure as snow
The people are relaxed, which is precious, you know
You have never been, you have to come and see
A special place that is very dear to me
God's country is how it is known
To me, fortunately, it is my home

# Being Me

Those who have it all, really don't have much
They have their individualism, no materials and such
In your heart is where you live your life now
You don't really need to understand how
It just did happened by opening my eyes
You've finally quit living that life of lies
Being yourself for all it's worth
For you have a short time on this earth.

# Sharing

Last night brought back pain I haven't
Felt in years
Today it brought to my eyes many
Tears.
Sharing what rock bottom was leaking
Through my eyes
They experienced with me many
Lows and highs
I have a way of shedding real
Light on things
Now they knew what a belief
Really means
To be able to look deeper than
One's skin
They will have their visions
To the end

# Theft of my Soul

I use to trust all people
Until the other day
Someone stole my worldly possessions
Just took them away
My first reaction was denial
Not willing to see
That someone that does not know
Took this part of me
I now have to rebuild because
It is gone
One day it will haunt this person
That did me wrong
Yes we all have made mistakes on
One another
It initially affected me but it will
Live forever with the other

# State of Consciousness

What I like most about writing
Each day
Is that you can teach people
That is far away
Understanding myself helps other
People see
What opening up your mind can allow
You to be
When I was down and out, friends
Came to my aid
They showed me I could survive and
Not to be afraid
Now it is my turn to give
This all back
I have made it, so can you
That is a fact
To a state of mind that is peaceful
As sleep
May you find yours forever to keep

# My Space, My Way

I am not happy when certain
People invade my space
It is best I know ahead
Just to save face
Others I like when they intrude
On me
Shining pleasant light on whatever
Maybe
Certain people have a way of causing
Us grief
Others bring to your life so much
Relief
You tell me which ones you would
Rather be around
Fortunately, for me, I had already
Found
That I enjoy happiness with those
Who hold the light
It makes life easier each and
Every night

# Avoiding the Pace

As the rain falls at a calm and gentle
Pace
Everyone around me seems to be in a
Race
Always trying to beat that
All-important time
I just watch them go by as I
Continue to rhyme
For I have found a way to pull out
Of that race
What you read now best represents
That case
I now don't have the need to out
Do you all
For in these words I found my
my beckoning call

# Why

Ours is not to know the answer
is to why
Just to enjoy this life and
bestow the high
For everything should happen without
Question or pause
God has given us each a purpose
And cause
Ours is to know what we want
Out of life
Take the opportunity to sharpen
The knife
Then cut away all that does
Not belong
Who's to say what is right
Or wrong
For I am here for you
As you for me
Why, I don't know, I just
Love the

# ♡pen Up

An ♡pen minds is a blessing
In disguise
Having experience ♡ne make us
M♡re wise
If we are cl♡sed, we live in
The dark
Never kn♡wing what it feels like t♡ have
An ♡pen heart
Sharing and caring with every♡ne we meet
Will make us, as individuals
Live m♡re c♡mplete
Seeing, hearing and listening
T♡ all
Making a c♡nsci♡us decisi♡n n♡t
All♡wing ♡ne t♡ fall
Makes f♡r a better place f♡r
All t♡ exist
♡pen your mind why m♡st
Y♡u resist

# Blessing In Disguise

Today I live with abundance
Of love
For I found that God up above
Before that was possible
I had to find me
Opening my heart allowed me
To see
That there is a spirit inside of
Us all
Some find it fast, others must fall
When you are ready to see the light
Give up resistance and give up the fight
God will be here to forgive your sin
Allowing us all the opportunity to win
That special feeling that only comes
From within
You will make it
God bless you my friend

# Thank You

We are all good at giving advice
Being able to take it
Makes us more wise
I enjoy being praised for the good
Things I do
And so should each and every one
Of you
A sense of accomplishment and the
Recognition we deserve
Is a feeling so wonderful that you
Have served
Both yourself and the God that
You love
How wonderful it is when you both
Rise above
Together as one things seem to glide
Right along
Because you are finally where
You belong

It is a rarity to get such help and guidance
Handed your way
The entire group of people making life
Easy each day
I find my happiness in all that I do because
He is here
Without belief in spirit, my smile
May turn to fear
The feelings of joy that God does bring into
My already happy heart
Is a feeling I wish upon everyone this is
Looking for a new start
Combining children and God with a
Strong family system
You will have a never ending situation and
A group willing to listen
The bottom line to happiness and a life
Worth living each day
Is friends, children, family and a God
To show you the way

Because I Care

The best gift I can give is that
♡f my hand
I extend t♡ every♡ne acr♡ss this
Great land
Helping ♡thers realize h♡w w♡nderful
They can be
Makes the l♡ve gr♡w inside
♡f me
F♡r all ♡f us need t♡ feel
Self-w♡rth
S♡me l♡se it ♡n the day
♡f birth
It is never t♡♡ late t♡ turn
It all ar♡und
Just ♡pen y♡ur heart and l♡♡k
What y♡u've f♡und
An incredible p♡wer s♡urce that
Is always here
♡pen the d♡♡r and let Him
Take the fear

# Bottom Line

You can become whatever you want if you
Put your mind in gear
The only obstacle I can see that will get in
Your way is fear
When I say go to any length to get what is
Your desire
It means grabbing a match and paper and
Literally starting a fire
By focusing in on who I am and the
Qualities I possess
I see I have chosen a career in which I will
Have and
The kids make it easy each day to hit the floor
With gleam
When you see their shining faces
You will know exactly what I mean
All my mentors have been so kind
The old ones and the new
To each teacher I have been in touch with
I say thank you

# To answer your Question

I have never made better decisions than
The ones I am making now
It wonderful to have a clear conscience
Let me show you how
We have a tendency to get caught up
In a world of make believe
Back to the basics is where our life
Really should retrieve
Bring back the Belief System into our
Children and home
For this is the only way not to live
Life alone
Get rid of all phoniness, don't be a hypocrite
That's right, what you see is exactly
What you get
No need for false pretenses, no need
To wear a disguise
I can assess your integrity by looking
In your eyes
Give an honest effort in all that you do
No one will ever question whether the things you say are
true

# Seeing is Believing

It seems so natural to share
From within
Others hide feelings they hold them
All in
What a joy to see changes within
A friend
You know by helping, you'll be together
To the end
Life's many treasures start deep inside
Open up and hang on, you are going
For a ride
To a place filled with joy with love and
With care
Don't worry my friend, I will help
You there
You are not alone in the way that
You feel
Others have already climbed that enormous hill

# Being You and only You

As your lips move up your weary face
A smile somehow does replace
These old feelings that use to be apart
Is rejoiced as love enters your
Heart
Wow, isn't it great to explore
Life's gifts
Taking what you want and away
The rest drifts
I've never been happier
And self-content
All the pain somehow, somehow
Just went
Gone forever; this smile will not
Leave
For now in myself, I do believe

## My Brother

For many years I felt this part of my life
Did not exist
Sharing our affection towards each other
We both did resist
I want to get to know you and understand
How you think
To our relationship, there is no time
This is the missing link
Recently it is different, you have shown
Me you care
In the past, seeing you was an occasion
That was rare
Now I am home to start a new career
I went to say thank you for your interest
And listening ear
You encouragement and words of advice
Mean a lot to me
For you are my brother and that
Will always be

# You are to Me...

I feel love in my heart like I have
Never felt before
It runs deep inside me, as deep as
The ocean floor
For you have shown me what it is
Suppose to be like
Together as one we will continue
Our hike
Where this is going only the wind
Does know
Let's learn from this and continue
To grow
No one person has ever made me
Feel
That someone other than me can be
This real
You are on my mind every moment
Of the day
And when I sleep, these thoughts
Don't go away

Nothing on this earth can ever take
You from me
We were meant to be together
That is plain to see
When you look at me, I see a
Certain spark
That could light up this earth
No matter how dark
The touch of your hand is as
Gentle as snow
Yet warms my heart
Just watch it glow
I had enjoyed each moment that we have shared so far
My friend, there is a lifetime
Filled with more

# Alternative

All this confusion going on around
Me
Somehow I still remain in complete
Serenity
When things like this use to come
About
I would bounce off the walls near
Freaking out
Since I have found that wonderful
Inner peace of me
Things come and go a little more
Naturally
Although I feel the pain, it is easy
To digest
I guess I am better off than
All the rest
We have not found a better way
To channel all the pain
My soul cleansed by God as the
Earth is by rain

Go ahead, give it a try, although
It may hurt
As we look down inside our souls
Cleaning out all the dirt
The pain we must suffer to gain
All our happiness
Is worth the short time of agony and sadness

# Turning It Over

The final step was just completed
To pave the path ahead
It is now out of my hands and into
His instead
I have done all I can to complete
What needed to be
Now for the process; to wait it out
And see
Since I knew exactly what it is
I want to do
No matter what they say, it will
Happen thru and thru
My feelings will not change as I'm
Put to the test
Becoming a teacher will happen
I know I will be the best
Settling for anything less would
Be a crying shame
For I have put my best effort forward
And have no one else to blame

Reflecting Back

As I read my book of poetry
I find it tells a tale
Of all my growing up to the finding
Of this made
When it all started, I never dreamed
It would be
A progression of a life, isn't it strange
That it is me
More so than that, I have learned a lot
About emotions
As I write about the trees, the flowers
And the oceans
Being able to share my life and my
Thoughts with you
Is a gift God has given, I realize
To a very few
If I could give each of you a gift
I would encourage you to write
Opening up your mind and hear will
Give you much insight

Keeping the Faith


You were here to help me
Yet unaware, my friend
The needs that you have written
Come thru in the end
For some unknown reason on
My headboard they were
When I needed help, I knew I
Could turn to her
A dire emergency case to determine
My fate
Thank God for existing at a previous
Date
This goes to show you what faith
Can do
When you believe in God, he is
There for you
The instrument in which He chose
To make it happen here
Has you my friend, so faithful and
So pure

# Reunited with Robbie

My friend of youth will return with in
A few days
How I have missed him in so many
Ways
I fear our as reunion in that I am a
New man
Except all these real changes, if you
Truly is my friend
We have so much to catch up on
So many new thoughts to share
I just want you to understand I am here
For you, I care
As I look back on all that
We have done
Every time we were together, we created
Our own fun
Thru good times and bad for each other
We have been
I can't wait for the reunion of His family
And my friend

# Procrastination

My biggest weakness is that I
Procrastinate
I look to help others, my needs
Can wait
Sometimes that put off can get me
Deep in the hole
Waiting until the last moment
Thinking it is no trouble
Now that I see what needs to
Be done
Put myself first make me number one
If this doesn't happen, all else
Will fall by
Be left with nothing but a towel
To cry
Get done what needs to be first and
For most
Then you can be the world's best host

# Walking

It is time to take that step
And see
What God really has instore
For me
Where to go, what to do
With God as my leader
I will be true
I will listen to His words
And walk In His shoes
I am the lucky one that He
Did choose
To carry this message here
And away
Sharing this love and listen
You may
For this is an honor and I feel
That is true
That God has chosen me to share
With you
He is never wrong and make

A mistake
Finally my heart is here
And awake
Being able to give comes easy
For me
Being able to receive, I will
Soon see
For I am willing to receive all of
His love
If he sends me a message
From above
I will walk the walk and talk
The talk? Being a messenger is sure
Going to be wild

# Listening

Two ears and one mouth in direct proportion
They should be used
Not letting yourself see this is to me, self-abuse
There is a lot we must hear before
We begin to speak
Listen to what is being told to you
Then begin to speak
It is nice to hear good things
Said about us all
But if our mouth is open, it is
Possible to fall
Then when all is heard and is
Filtered though
Should we begin to speak
But only what is true
For having only one mouth and
these two ears
Listen twice as much, there is a lot
To hear

# Enlightenment

The most true to God's spiritual awakening
I have ever felt
Into my soul, Jesus Christ did
Melt
My arms went straight up high in
The sky
The felt the omnipresence of His
Staring eyes
My limbs were like air or even
Thinner yet
I feel as if I finally reality has
Set
That all mighty God who has been
Introduced to me
A bonding of flesh, I now became
We All thanks to a day filled with spiritual love
Sent down from Heaven
You are my lord above

# Getting to Know You

It is ok to take some time to be alone
With you
Not being lonely, just understand
Who
Each of us really are, different in our
Own way
The uniqueness of individuals
Mine is love to stay
The time I have by myself just to think
Things through
Is very important for my life
And then to share it with you
Because really, all we ever have is
What exists inside
That and good old God up above
To Him I do confided
So take some time to yourself
And learn who you are
Life is short; it is here
Make it stretch real far

Man of all Men

Go ahead spirit, grow inside of
My soul
Make me a man both pure and
Whole
Be free of fears; let down that
Guard
It matters how difficult, we matter
How hard
A feeling of freedom only comes from
Within
Put down your eye, and confide
In Him
It's ok to be happy, footloose
And fancy free
This is the spirit of God alive
Inside of me
If you need a hand, I'll lead
You my heart
God will take away that unwanted
Part

# In the Beginning

My heart and soul are filled with
Love, happiness and joy
Today I'm crawling as if I were a
Little boy
Leaning this walk is going to take time
To understand it all
With God on my side I can not
Fall
Just show me what it is, my Lord
That you have for me
Sharing and caring with others that
Is plain to see
There has to be more to it
More to it thru and thru
Now that I Have turned my life over
To the care of you
Just give me what it is, my Lord
Shine the light on the place
Let me see a sparkle on every
Child's face
You my friend, have shown me what
It is like to live
Now with my new life, I have turned it to you to give

# Learning New Ways

I learn something new about myself
Each and every day
Whoever I am
I seem to be on my way
Where this journey is going does not
Really matter
I am now the pitcher and my spirit
Is the batter
So when I threw my ideas up his
Heavenly way
He hits me back a message
Pointing to the right way
By finding who I am, whatever
That may be
I am able to be conscious,
I can finally see
That there is another life
Inside this physical being
The spirit is in my heart, I can hear
It is my singing
Thank you, my friend, for being
There when really needed be
Letting me get to know who I am and
the opportunity to serve thee

# Mom of all Moms

My mom is so loving and caring with
The world's largest heart
They all have this in common that one little
Certain part
When you're down, when you're sick or
Just need a hug
Or need a place to sleep when
You're feeling like a lug
Always a good word or advice or a
Smile, ever so bright
That you can keep with you each
And every night
They have this special attachment
They will never let you go
They love you for who you are
Not who you know
This special person that I am
Describing to you
Is a mom so wonderful, beautiful
Unique and true
To this special woman I owe a
Thank you in Bold
For in my heart, a special place
You will always hold

# A Better Way

Work, work, work, and work
Some more
If this is your life, what a
Bore
Take a look at the trees, the flowers
And the plants
Look at the finest things that
Love does enhance
The earth we live on offers many
Wonderful days
From the beauty of the sea
To the bright sun rays
Wake up tomorrow and look in
The mirror
Open your mind as well as
Your ear
A message that awaits you with a
Wonderful gift
A new beginning, for you today
A spiritual uplift

# A Spring Day

Spring is in the air as the flowers
Blossom bright
Lighting up our faces at their beautiful
Sight
The roses and their colors, their beauty
And their scent
Telling you to stop and smell them, take
Their little hint
The air is crisp and clean as I wake
From my nightly rest
I enjoy all the seasons, but Spring
I like the best
The birds sing their little songs and
The grass turns ever so green
A little Spring shower decides to come
Help and clean
Being able to enjoy a moment with all
Of God's gifts
All the day today pressure it really
Does lift
Won't you join me in a session of
Seeing a day of Spring
There are so many pleasures to your
Life it will bring

# A Message from God

If God could write a letter
He would send it thru me
Tell her, my friend, to put her
Faith in thee
Let my child know that the only way
She can deal
Turn it over to me, I am for real
Your prayers are being heard and the
Message is clear
The position you are in as my child
Is safe and secure
I know times are tough but you
Continue to fit
Turn it over to me, don't try and
Fix it
Follow the plan I have set forth
For you
Remember you're number one
Not number two

# Being Considerate

Nothing really ever seems to go just
As planned
It seem we are right on time and
Have to hold everyone else's hand
I do not mind it when I make
Myself late
It really irritates me when others
Make me wait
Not in a hurry, just on my own
Clock
At my pace, not yours, I choose to
Do my walk
Take into consideration how someone
Else may feel
Hold up your end, let them know you
Are for real
Thank you for being more considerate
And thinking your commitment thru
It makes for a better relationship
Between I and you

# It's Worth it All

The environment we live in is
Extremely stressed out
Everywhere we go people seem
To always shout
Reversing that role is left up
To you
Decide where you want to be and
With who
Our time on earth is a relatively
Short stay
Make your life worth living each
And every day
Fulfill your dream and see
They come true
No matter what others say, it is
Up to you
To take this gift that God
Has given
Because your life is worth livin'

# Huhn

The confusion in my head is running as
Wild as Niagara Falls
Overflowing with emotions is not comfortable
With them all
I have all this love that I don't understand
For male, for female and especially
For the land
I pray about it and wonder if I've
Gone too far
Just look at yourself and remember
Where you are
Know no limits, explore all walks of
Your choice
Let everyone hear this love in
Your voice
Don't be scared of feeling
A bit out of place
Do what you can to help our
Dying human race

# Acceptance

Why am I torn about this new
Life I choose
Or is it that I set myself
Up to lose
Don't beat yourself up and let others
Be your judge
Live for yourself and never
Hold a grudge
If I choose to believe in a
Concept called God
Does not mean I expect others to follow my prod
Only encourage, educate and teach
Out to everyone your hand should reach
So let go of the knot reality
Is staring you in the face
Turn your questions into answers and
Help this human race

# Love?

My friend asked me today to
Define the word love
A difficult question, that one
Asked above
I wrote earlier about

Love of all kinds
But as I read it, it does not
Define
To me love is a feeling that
I can't get enough of
I "like" a lot, but few I "love"
To truly define such a word
As this
You have to have experience this
Feeling of bliss
I know in my heart what the
Real meaning should be
Love is what you get when
You get to know me

# God

The more I give faith in God
Up above
The easier it becomes to except
How to love
Things that I wish for do somehow
Come true
Since I have turned my life over
To you
The little things come easy and
The big ones are fine
I let them out of my soul and
Into thine
Each day I walk, I find Him
To be there
Making life a joy each and
Everywhere
The life I was looking for
I really did find
It was in my backyard
This entire time

# Subbing for Mrs. Potter

The 1st hour is done quite loud I
Might say
Bouncing off the walls, Mr. Hartwick, can
We play
Looking forward to silence and watch
Their minds work hard
Then out for a run around the old
School yard
Rebecca broke her ship and was in
Tears for fear
"Do I have to go home or can I just
Stay here"
Mrs. Robinson came in and put down the
The iron claw
It lasted just briefly as do most
Laws
Finally lunch is here only four minutes
They wait
I had to display leadership by making them
Be quiet and late
Back to class wound up and ready to
Speak
Outside with Norman not Another peep

# What Happened to Peace

What is this world coming to
The violence that exists
People forget what it is like to love
Instead they just resist
Our leaders of this country have fallen
By the side
I do not know one of them in which
I would confide
Someone needs to take a hold
Before it is too late
We are destroying our environment
At an alarming rate
More concern is being given to
Oil and its price
Then there is being giving for the sacred
Human life
Many different areas contribute to
The current mess at hand
Like watching it on television instead
Of experience it on land
We all need to slow it down and

Look at ourselves
Time to take out a towel and dust
Off all the shelves
Wouldn't this be a better place
If we all gave a smile
It would make life enjoyable
At least for awhile
The answer to my question of
Who should take control
Is God up above for he will
Let you know
He has not left our country
Our country left Him
When you learn, what I already know
Then our world will win

# Pick Yourself Up

Life has many ups and downs
More so than steady pace
You head and heart strings are pulling
In a constant race
Never a quiet knowing what to think
About others all around
I am always wondering in your mind
What is going down
People do and say the most
Outrageous things
Pain and agony or love and happiness
To each other it brings
I always try to be the latter
In all of my affairs
I find people feel loved if they
See that someone cares
Next time I am on one of those
Cerebral roller coasters
I'll pull out my happy shooters
From that ever present holster

# Nieces

One is named Leah Michelle, the other
Is Deja Lynn
The older is calm and collected, the younger
A whirlwind
Two of the most precious lives God has
Ever given
They make each day of my life worth
Living
We have a wonderful relationship, always
Laughing and having fun
Tickling and flipping and chasing on the
Run
What a wonderful gift for my brother
And his wife
Not one, but two, they have blessed
My life
God, please hold them all in your
Arms ever so tight
Giving them a wonderful life, making
Sure they are always alright

May 20, 1992

Today my heart aches; there is a lot
Going on
Deja's on the mind from my awaking
At dawn
Having to be in a place that I am not
Ready for
Rather, I would be on a bike in the
Great outdoors
My head is in the clouds, my heart
Is still in the class
Lighten up, let it go, enjoy them
Have a blast
My nerves are wearing thin, my
Patience doing the same
Wild, restless, very untamed
Lesson learned not all have control
Not a moment today that was dull

# There for Me

In time of need, when the situation at
Hand was rough
You were there for me, you helped me be
Real tough
With the spirit of God, you so gracefully
Express
Making that day much easier, allowing my
Mind to rest
I thank you for your thoughts, your care
And you concern
It is no wonder from you I have
learned
What it is to love, to share with all
Around
It is no wonder from you my spirituality
Was found
Time and time again, you are there
For thee
I want you to know how much my
Friend you really mean to me

# A Moment with Friends

I spent last weekend with a lot of people
New friends and old
A moment short lived for a lifetime
I can hold
We all met and chatted, laughing with one
Another
While the new ones and I got to know each other
Then, it was just us guys in hand to hand
Competition
On the golf course to have some fun
That was our ambition
Jeff lost his glasses, atypical for
This young man
Put a damper for a moment on the
Situation at hand
With a little humor and a lot of exchanging
Verbal warfare
We found out over time that we all still
Do care
Friends, true friends will last forever
And a day
It is sad that we all have to part
Our own way

# Getting to Know You

Treating you like a lady makes me feel
Like a man
Our age has nothing to do with the
Situation at hand
As I sit in class, you are in my thoughts
Not just once or twice, this happens a lot
I like what I see in you, we seem to
Communicate well
I would like to learn more about you
Only time will tell
Being with you is so comfortable, when you
Are away, you are here
I keep a mental picture of your beauty
My dear
The moment we first kissed, I felt this
Twang in my heart
Hoping our lips would never have to part
I would like to see you more, to learn
What makes you, you
Until I see you again, I hope the
Moments are few

# It's Time

I am now ready to settle down and have a
Family of my own
Several kids a dog, white picket fence,
And a home
I feel I am mature enough and on the
Right track
To share with others, with the right
Woman, never looking back
I knew why I am both in soul and
In mind
In search for the right one, I will soon
Find
I have all this love I want to
Give away
No more saving it for a rainy day
God, please give me the one you
Have directly picked out
For if you send her to me, I will
Know without a doubt

# Double Vision

When my day starts off with a prayer
And a smile
Makes getting out of bed really
Worth while
Some kids playing and some are
In deep thought
Using their minds with resistance, I
Won't let them wrought
In the back of all my thoughts
Is this beautiful delicate smile
Belonging to a woman who is
Making each day worth while
The kids can really tell when you
Are having a good day
Laughs and joking, yet doing what
You say
As the day winds down and the
Kids go away
She still is on my mind, as she was
At the beginning of my day

# Tammy Lee

To me you are one of a kind
A vision of beauty inside my mind
My instincts tell me to find out more
My heart tells me that I adore
You are omnipresent in my every existence

Leading me on a path of least resistance
Every moment I can with you is a reward
Every moment we are apart, to seeing you
I look forward

# Recital

The girls are dancing, flipping and
Tapping
Friends and family in the audience clapping
What a joy it must bring to you and
Ms. Valley
It is show time, no more dilly dally
So up on stage, let the show
Begin
The grand finale, it all must
End
A lot of hard work and detailed
Patience put in
You have given us all a great
Pleasure, my friend
Without you at the helm, it all
May not have been
So smile and enjoy all the kids
And your kin

## Thinking Things Through

For us to resist how others want us to feel
Is right
To resist how we actually feel, is a necessary
internal fight
Our heads and hearts are always filled
With much confusion
To avoid reality is simply and illusion
We were given a mind to think rational
And true
Take your confusion and process it
Thru
Nothing worthwhile is easy
Take enough time
Either you will or will not end up
To find
What it is that you truly feel
And sincerely need
Nothing can grow until you
Plant the seed

# Reality

A question I am often asked is
I want to pick your mine
What are you looking for, what do you
Think you'll find
People often want to know this
Other side of me
What is it I have that you don't
What do you think you will see
People seem to relate to the words
I write
What is stopping you, give up
The fights
For we all possess these feelings that
I do talk about
Most of us deny ourselves with
Unnecessary doubt
So to want to pick my mind and know
The other side
Open up your eyes, my friend, no
Longer shall you hide
For this person I am talking about
Is a part of us all
I will help you stand, my friend, and not let you fall

# ♡mnismile

My goal in life is to find a way
To never be emotionally down
The sharing discovery, what it is that
I found
This is a big challenge, yet I seem to
Be on my way
I am becoming happier each and
Every day
By sharing my words with each
♡f you
I see others feel the same way
That I do
To be completely happy, I believe
It takes two
A spiritual relationship with God and
Getting to know you

# Thanks for Being Honest

Thanks for being honest on how it is
You feel
What a wonderful quality, that of being
Real
All though I have known you most of
My life
I am now looking at you in a
Different light
I really pray that someday I will
Find someone true
Who knows what God has in store
For me and you
Live each moment as easy and
Free
That seems to be overwhelming, yet
It is real to me
We all seem to put up shields to
Protect our loving heart
No longer will I allow anyone to tear
Me apart
To be your friend is a feeling I believe
To be true
Looking forward to further getting
To know you

# Don't Misunderstand Me

I must not give a good impression of
How it is I feel
People misread my intentions, they
Mistake for what is real
I must not give a good impression as
To whom I really am
A heart as big as life, I care about
My friends
I really am a caring person for all
Of you that are in pain
I have been where you are,
The tears falling like rain
It angers me and pains me
When others generalize
I look at each of you as individuals
Because I realize that when I was the one
Who was in that state of mind
I misread everyone until I did find
That there are very few people who
Really do care
Don't push them aside
Realize and draw them near

# Live and Learn

I really should not concern myself with
What others think or say
People will hurt each other to make
Themselves feel a certain way
For one to judge another simply by
What they hear
Is a superficial stigma yet common
I fear
I do not like to fall victim to
Simple small talk
If you want to know me, ask me,
Then listen as we walk
Letting others form your opinion
Is real sign of being insecure
The only truth you'll ever find
Is that of being pure
Although no one is perfect
In our lives for that we stride
Just because one sees you as less
That is no reason to hide

The Choice is Yours

I do not like to be shined especially
By a friend
Are not they supposed to stick together
To the bitter end
I feel as if I am a disease and you
Are the cure
A lifetime of companionship definitely changing I fear
If I have done something other then
Be me
Open up and strive for honesty
Is the key
I feel as if I am not wanted, that
I make you feel on the edge
Yet I thought a long time ago our
Friendship we did pledge
The ball is in your court, decide
Without a doubt
You can hit in, my friend, or you
Can hit it out

One Giant Step

For the last 8 weeks have been
Quite a blur
First learning from him, then learning
From her
Two of the finest teachers I have
Been around
Off to the teacher prep Program
I am finally bound
I learned a lot about my profession
And what it is we do
They teach to us; and also learn
From you
The prospects in the class for the
most part where in touch
To one, although a lot to be desired
I do leave much
The first class I received the "A"
I so needed to achieve
Dale gave me a second chance,
In him I do believe

Maureen is very excited about
When it is she shares
You can tell she loves people
Just by the way she cares
The drive each day is a
Way to unwind
For myself, lately, the only time
I find
Each day the elk are at the
Farm basking in the sun
I can always count on seeing
At least just one
If you have never seen a Redwood
As I do each day
You need to take a little time and
Drive up my way
To your right or to your left
There are giants all around
I live in the presence of the only
One's ever found

Each day there are bikes riding this
Beautiful road
This whole experience came about
Because I was to teach
Just like Dale did to me, but my
Hand will reach
Another piece of road is paved toward
My current goal
Becoming a teacher is a big part
Of my soul
Now it is time to break to finish
What need be
Just another part of life I am
Getting to know as me
I would like to say thanks to all
Who opened the door
I will return the favor
For now and ever more

# Regret

I ran from her this girl
I loved with all my heart
I have made a mistake
I hope forever we do not part
I just shared with her what it was
I felt
My eyes did water, my heart did
Melt
How could I be so blind
It is plain to see
That my heart shattered the
Blame it on my
Not too many things in my life
That I have regret I have done
By far this experience is regret
Number One
You did forgive me
I am sorry and in pain
Yet the love of my life
You will always remain

# A Degree

For three years I have waited for
Principles and I stand
Finally a diploma I hold in my
Hand
From the day I walked across that
Centosure Stage
Someone told me I did not qualify
What on an outrage
We went round and round
I was sure I was right
And when I am, I continue to
Fight
I take the classes she suggested
not one did any good
Another year gone by with no
Diploma I stood
Everyone doubting me as if
I have not even gone
Once again I had to prove myself right and
everyone else's doubt wrong
Now I have closed a chapter
Which brings much relief
You can accomplish whatever you
Want if in you, you do have belief

# I ♡ffer You...

You can g♡ ♡n living your life
In pain and ag♡ny
♡r have a lifetime filled with
Happiness and s♡me♡ne like me
What s♡me♡ne else is causing
Is killing the ♡nes wh♡ l♡ve you
Put that smile back ♡n your beautiful
Face f♡r that pers♡n is thru
N♡ l♡nger shall y♡u have t♡ relate
T♡ pain bey♡nd n♡ end
F♡r awaits y♡u is s♡me♡ne wh♡ cares
Y♡ur family and friend
Remember what it is like t♡ fall
In l♡ve
N♡t the pain ♡f falling ♡ut
Let that rise ab♡ve
F♡r the first feeling is happiness
The better ♡f the tw♡
This is the ♡ne I d♡ wish
Up♡n you

# Give and Return

Strangers of all walks
Sharing this part of me
The way they are reacting
In what it is they read
I feel as if I had finally found
That one certain part
The ability to express myself
What is really in my heart
People saying to me that what I
Am doing is right
Telling them not to be scared
That they should try and write
To know that I really can help others
See their pain
Let them know they're not alone
That I have felt the same
A feeling I can hold for the
Rest of my days
To know I have helped others
In so many ways
Is a special gift that you
Give me in return
For together are both?

# Sense of Accomplishment

The day is coming soon to start
My new career
A long journey ahead and a mind
That is clear
Given opportunity because of how I
performed in the past
Will soon allow me the chance at
My own class
To set a goal and watch it come true
Thru hard work and dedication
It can happen to you
My heart filled with joy
My face filled with smile
My pride filled with completion
It has been awhile
Yet time is all relative
It is never too late
Go after your goals
No longer shall you wait

# Tonight

You never know when to express yourself
To tell who you really are
Some people might say that you have
Gone too far
I believe in being honest
Just tell how it is
Like this truth session I'm having with
Jon, Marilyn and Liz
We all have things in common that
We will never know
Like sharing our emotions
Just letting them go
It is a way of expressing ourselves
Just being you
It is these I share with who really
Understand for I feel
Don't be scared with what is real

# Heart Strings

It seems as if you have grabbed my heart strings
And never even know
That I am pulling on yours, wanting to be
With you
I understand your situation with this
Young man
I want you to know I am here for you
I extend you my hand
Don't hold yourself responsible for
How others feel
Be true to yourself and what you
Feel is real
A smile takes over my face when I think
Of you
Holding you in my arms
I enjoy to do
You have so much to offer to a life joy
Your warm tender heart makes me feel
Like a little boy
I can only hope you feel the same as
It is I do
I await in anticipation until the next time I see you

# Patiently I Wait

You have a sense of humor to match your
Beautiful smile
It makes getting to know you
Worth all the while
I hope you can see how it is
I do feel
When I look in your eyes
What I see is real
When you're in my presence
I get all giddy inside
Then I pray to see if this is right
For in Him I do confide
From tears to laughter and everything
In between
You are worth the wait, my friend,
Whether long or short
For it is you, someday, I would like
To court

# Joint Effort

I want to be with you
That is plain to see
Do away with your pain and sorrow
Come be with me
For what I have to offer you is a lifetime
Filled with love
To rid yourself of all your pain
Confide in God above
If you choose to remain
It will always be the same
Constant frustration and ongoing game
I will wait for a while but a lifetime
Is too short
It is now you I say it again
That I would like to court
Take some time to think things thru
And decide what's right
For in my eyes and my heart
You are a beautiful sight

# I'm Honored

I have shared my recent work with
Just a very few
Today it happened, a dream come
True
A fancy lady named Brooke was given
A task to achieve
For at her age poetry comes difficult
I do believe
Given my choices in which to
Conquer this task
Confiding in her mother
Which one I do ask
Here are some books
Pick one that suits you
Narrowing it down to just a few
I am honored she is quoting
One of my own
I feel as if I have finally
Known
That sharing my life in
Paper and ink
Gives even the young amount
To thin

# Inundated

I feel as if the flood gates have
Opened full force
Inundated with a great deal of work
In each and every course
It is time to put aside all other
Forms of thought
Dedicate all my time to this career
I've sought
Maintain a steady head and a clear
State of mind
The light at the end of the tunnel
We all shall soon find
Instead of worrying about the load
That feels like a ton of lead
Do what is necessary to get
Yourself ahead
In the end of this time that seams
So heavy and fast
A teacher in the classroom
I will be at last

# Perseverance

Sometimes in life we are faced with a
Great task
To succeed or to fail, to you I do ask
Some say maybe, I just might
Be able to
This is not me but, is it you
Others say I will, no matter what it takes
True to definition - no, maybes or
Fakes
This desire to be, to never
Give in
Is a burning admiration in life
To win
At the end of the rope
When you're hanging by a thread
Conquer that moment, perseverance,
Move ahead

# Mistakes

To go ahead and do what you feel in your
Heart is wrong
A feeling of disarray to you only
It does belong
A mistake knowingly made is hard to
overturn
Just like any mistake from it you must
Learn
Look into your soul, to where your
Forgiveness button lies
Turn it from off to on
For you only get more wise
If you never made mistakes
Never crash and burn
This thing called life, about it you
Wanted now learn
Don't be so hard on yourself for the
Mistake that was made
Live and learn from them all, no need
To be afraid

# Please Stop

To sit and watch a child hurt for
Love inside
To confront his apparent discomfort
In which he does hide
Is beyond my realm of thought
Beyond my sense of love
I do pray for him to God up above
I cannot stand by and let this
Abuse exist
I will fight the system
To his happiness I will persist
My heart cries out for those who
Have no choice
I will speak up for those who have
Lost their voice
To give all I have to a heart that
Has turned to stone
So maybe, one day, he can
Smile alone

# Tenderness

Although it ? awhile for us to
Share our thoughts
We found out in comman
We do have a lot
It excites me to get to know you
A little more each day
A smile comes to my face
Even when you are away
Also I think of you
I can't help but see
Your beautiful brain, eyes staring right
Back at me
I see your tender heart filled with love
Ever so kind
You have all of these traits that
Are so hard to find
The first night we spent
I hoped would never end
Deep thoughts and feelings to each
Other we did lend
When our lips met
Under the starlit night
Holding you in my arms felt ever so right

# I have a Dream

I have a burning desire to
Write music and sing
A constant thought that in my head
Does ring
I know I have the feeling deep
Inside my heart
This it takes to make it happen
To set myself apart
Looking at the people who are
Expressing themselves aloud
The energy they must possess
The "high" that is above the clouds
This something that is so inviting
I want to feel that "high"
That can only come from doing
Your best, not just getting by
Give it a shot, see if a dream will
Come true
I will do the writing
The rest will come fro

# Life's Many Treasurers

The sparkle of a diamond
The grace of a swan
The way the dew shines as the sun
Hits it at dawn
The beauty of a wave as it rolls
Into shore
The power of a lion
As it lets out a roar
The speed of a cheetah
The size of a whale
The little puppy dog that is
Wagging its tail
Nature has to offer us some many
Wonderful sights
If you see it all being ruined
Do what you feel is right
If you just stand by and let
Those sights be destroyed
Consider that a contribution to the problem
Not a means to avoid

# Fragile Heart

Falling for you has happened
So fast
I have been hurt so often
From those in the past
Sorry for feeling insecure about the way
You feel
They have all said the same
Turned out not to be real
When you are around
I feel so warm inside
I have put away any shield
Let my heart out for a ride
I may express anger, frustration and fear
Only because I am scared, my dear
Please be gentle
I have a fragile heart
It is best you know this
From the very start

# Nature Walk

About a mile as an eagle flies
Is a breath of fresh air
Surrounded by giants, as gentle as
Life, each and everywhere
Enjoying the sharing of friendly thoughts
with a very bright young mind
A little in common, a lot I learned
From her I did find
Strolling through nature, across a bridge
Protecting a precious creek
A wonderful place to relieve the stress
That comes to us each week
Look around in all directions
The life that exists today
How could anyone want to cut and clear
It all away
Thanks to you for sharing with me
This place just like my home
A get-away, a reality check
When I want to be alone

# It will Happen

I sit and wonder for hours, upon days
About that certain one
Wishing upon a falling star to find
Her and be done
Each relationship I encounter
Gets a fair and speedy trial
Some, my last, for a walk on the beach
Others go on for quite awhile
At times I felt that rush of blood
Sent directly to my heart
It seems like so few ticks go by
Before we have to part
There have been a few that includes
That has vanished into thin air
I only wish I could get them back
It seems to be me only fair
No more looking no more searching
Sit back and just wait
It will happen either by love, by luck
Or by good old fate

# Let it ♡ut

Butterflies fluttering in my stomach at the speed
♡f a hurricane
Should I ♡r should I n♡t
Remains t♡ be the same
With each breath that I d♡ take
C♡mes a sense ♡f readiness
Until I walk d♡wn the r♡ad
I will c♡ntinue t♡ sec♡nd guess
I feel uneasy like a skiff afl♡at
A st♡rmy lake
It g♡es away when I sleep yet
Returns when I d♡ wake
T♡ c♡ntinue t♡ cause myself
The feeling ♡f disc♡ntent
Is n♡t c♡nsiderate ♡f wh♡ I am
N♡r is it time well spent
Grab a h♡ld ♡f y♡urself as if you
You were ab♡ut t♡ fly
Treat th♡u like a king ♡r queen
T♡ him ♡r her d♡ n♡t lie
Make a p♡int t♡ let it g♡
S♡ar like a bird in flight
Y♡u will find letting it ♡ut
Y♡u will end that unnecessary fight

# Clearing the Clouds

I find that people hide their feelings
Like a groundhog on his day
For some ungodly reason they think
They will just go away
Please my friend, realize your pain and
Find a panacea drug
Even if it is just a teddy bear
Offering up a heartwarming hug
Don't you know the simple things get you
Thru the hardest times
Like the sound of something
Piano accompanying, a hymn or a rhyme
Maybe even a friendly visit from a special
Child's smile
Or a walk on a chilly beach that goes
On for miles and miles
Let these feelings that are buried
Rise like fresh baked bread
Clear the clouds in your heart and
The roller coaster in your head
Release all tension into the air
Like a hot air balloon in flight
Imaging yourself gleaming with joy
As a star does late at night

# Christmas

Christmas is a day filled with
Love and joy
A day for me to feel like a
Young, little boy
Christmas is a day to celebrate
The birth of Jesus Christ
To smile and rejoice His wonderful
Life
Christmas is a day for family to
Share their love
To let all your problems just simply
Rise above
Christmas is a day for children
To wait for Santa to come
So they can play with all their new
Toys and has lots of fun
But most of all, Christmas is to me
A day of peace and love
As calm and gentle as the flight
Of a beautiful white dove

# Piano Man

If I could trade my finest attribute
The things I do the best
For a chance to play the piano like
George Winston and Dave Lantz
I listen to them make their notes
I close my eyes and see
Music flowing from finger to key
Like an eagle soaring free
I feel the melody and the rhythm
With the pounding of my heart
From highs to lows, they seem to
Fly from every piece and part
Sometimes it's as loud as thunder
Other times, soft as rain
Just a chance to create a sound
From that black and white plane
I want to turn all these feelings into music
That flows from my heart
The piano will be the tool as these
Two dimensions  do part

# Dear Friend

At times I look into thin air
Your image appears so bright
As if you are a beam of sunlight
Shining down so bold and light
From out of the blue, I feel you near
When you are nowhere to be found
I like the way you make me feel
So safe and so sound
We are together so very little
We talk secretive real late
In my heart and in my head
A place for you does wait
I seem to find you in my heart
Each time I do pray
A special person you are to me
May that never go away

# It is All Mine

Of all the questions asked
Each day how my answers do appear
A difference of opinion is
Spoken that is what you hear
Are there really answers to
Life's many trials
If you add them all up
They could be seen for miles
It seems only natural to
Take it all in
Listen to all the "answers" and
Decide in the end
Can someone else truly decide
What is right for you
Your answers should come from Him
The conceivable chilly real true
I feel that I am old enough
To separate reality from not
For what I possess deep inside
Is all I have really got

# I Like

I like music without words created
From the heart
I like the story of Moses
Making the water part
I like fresh air blown in from the
ocean shore
I like my time to be alone
Now even more
I like to be in a classroom to
Share all I can
I like the progression of watching
This boy become a man
I like to laugh and smile each
And everyday
I like to have all kinds of experiences
To learn a new way
I like to make others feel that they
Can also smile
I like to give my heart to those who have
Been hardened for awhile
But best of all I love my family
To them I give my heart
Unlike the story I mentioned above
I hope we never part

## The Game

The day is upon me, the challenge is near
As I venture off of my new found career
A leather sphere filled tightly
With air
Knowledge from many sources
I share
The young men's hearts are beating so fast
Their palms are ringing wet
I remain calm on the outside
Never let them see you sweat
Many hours have gone by in
Preparation for this day
May they work as a team and
At the same time
To watch these young men pour out
Their hearts to win
Just seeing these precious moments
With all my new found friends
This is what life is all about
A basket and a ball
No matter whether you win or lose
Just that you never fall

# Feelings

I am innocent, I was just standing by
To make another look so bad
I ask myself why
Are people really that jealous
Do they remain insecure
I am fortunate I feel as I do
About myself in?
I get upset when others take
Cheap shots at my expense
Don't they realize my ability to

I feel as if I am a survivor
In a world of make believe
On an island in the south Pacific
To Alaska, I should retreat
Please remember before you hurt
Someone or make them feel real low
That their feelings are at stake
You have no right to restrict their flow

# The End Results

Have you ever stopped to wonder
How deep you really reach
To all these impressionable minds
The information you do teach
Each receiving a lesson in life
At a different and separate pace
For the feedback we do need
As is written on their face
Isn't it strange how they retain more
By doing what they see
Why was this not the case when
They were teaching me
To find a way to get into
Each and every head
Not just discussing information in
The back they just read
For us as teachers to have really abandoned
Success inside our hearts
Is to see a child blossom in life
For that is where it really starts

# Kids

They always seem to know
Just how it is you really feel
There is no make belief
What you say to them is real
The sparkle in their eyes
The glisten in their cheeks
Will stay with you for an eternity
Not just one or two weeks
They always know when to give a hug
Their timing is just right
Especially when you have been up
Preparing most of the previous night
Letting in this world could change
What it is that I now do
Nothing seems as much to me as
Do all of you
What I am sharing with you are children
I love them all
Even if they disobey and run
Down the hall

# Marathon

The gun has sounded
and the race has begun
It seems like in a circle
I run, and run
My heart and soul have been given to
This very career
The current way of assessing us
Is scary, I fear
Someone seems to think that it takes
A high I.Q. to teach
I, for one, believe from our hearts
Is where we all should reach
Someone also is trying to stop me
Don't they understand
I will become a teacher
Somewhere across this great land
Like a few hundred meters
Run with hurdles all the way
To break the tape at the end
I will do someday

# Train Station

This career is like a train station
Never knowing what you will see
Not sure where they have been
Never knowing where they will be
A passenger on this trip
Just here for a little while
Growing and learning all about life
Then moving ahead one short mile
We are the conductors, the leaders
Of this train
Our job is to put knowledge into
Every little brain
We find that we have passages in
Every car on line
From the steam engine, to the caboose
May we expand each little mind
Just remember when they pull in
To treat them with respect
You would not want to see a train car of yours
End up in a wreck

# The Boys

It seems like only yesterday
That we all first met
Up and down our little court
Working up a sweat
Me not knowing what to do
Making it up as I go
It is amazing to watch you now
And how easily that you glow
There are many moments that come to mind
As I look back
The most is at Fortuna with 1-3-1 attack
You all have given me a thrill
A blessing in disguise
As I look at the intensity in each
One of your eyes
I only hope that I can keep up with you
This season in the sun
Because to me, each of you are
All number one

# Season Finale

What a way to end it all
In an event such as this
The shot is on its way
Sometimes you have to miss
One last time we take the floor
To play as a team
Let's hit it on the run with intensity
And eyes of gleam
The crowd is on their feet
To cheer you to a win
Coach and I are on the bench
Our help we do lend
It is all up to you
Bounce back and grab a hold
Play them to the end no matter if you're
Hot or cold
Just remember who you are
And where you all come from
Never should you think of yourselves
Less than number one

# A Poem Is

A poem is an expression of how you
Think and feel
A poem is the writing down of
Something that is real
A poem is a way to tell the world
Exactly who you are
A poem is a way to reach these people
Here and far
A poem can make you happy or
Make you shed a tear
A poem is a way to get over a
Real horrible fear
A poem can be for someone you
You really care about
A poem can cause a question
Of something you really doubt
But most of all, a poem is a way to
Help you remain on top
Take a pen in your hand and write
May you never stop

# If I Could...

If I could teach the world at once
Would it be a better place
Take away all the pain that exists
And with love I would replace
If I could teach the world at once
Would I have enough to say
Show every hurting child they have
Another way
If I could teach the world at once
And show them I have the keys
To rid us of all the war that exits and
Create some world peace
If I could teach the world at once
And share my open heart
Get the families back together
Do away with divorcing apart
If I could teach the world at once
Show a way to feed us all
There is no reason to have starvation
It is a tragic fall
If I could teach the world at once
Would it be a better plac

# There is a Time

There's a time to laugh
And there's a time to cry
There's a time to tell the truth
And, yes, a time to lie
There's a time to share
There's a time to hold back
There's a time things are said and done
That you wish you could retreat
There's a time to be a child
And a time to be mature
There's a time to feel like a "him"
And a time to feel like "her"
There's a time you ask why
And a time you know
There's a time to hang on
And a time to let go
There's a time to express yourself
And a time to be quiet
There's a time to be a spectator
And a time to start a riot
But most of all there is a time
To be who it is you are
Unlike all the other times take this one quite fa

# Grading

It was an "A", thank God,
The first grade I had to give
There for a moment
I wondered if I'd live
It felt real tense to actually
Grade another's I.♡.
How did you feel when it first
Happened to you
All that work and time well spent
Just to receive an "A"
It seems to me, to reward them
There must be a better way
Than to put into words how it is
I see your child
In a space on sheet
In a file that's been compiled
I feel the need to communicate
To each mom and dad
Eye to eye, heart to heart,
About their lass and lad
To really grade another's performance
You must be willing to see
That no one is perfect Especially "me"

# Soon

As the final chapter begins to unfold
The cause is narrowing in
The long hard road comes to a halt
And another one does new begin
There is this race inside of my head
As if my brain was a type? Track
Plunging forward with tunnel vision
And never looking back
Each obstacle that seems to come up
Is that of "Satin's" dream
The will to teach will at last his thought
My life I will redeem
Through another hurdle
May I have legs enough to leap
Nothing can take away my dream
I have it for to keep
As an eagle falls from his next
He will eventually soar away
I will get what it is I want
It will happen soon one day

# School

What does school really mean
deep inside your heart
Why not try to build them up
Instead of tearing them apart
What does school really do for those
Who actually attend
If you make false promises
You only pretend
What do schools really teach
It is all from a book
Or is it from our actions
You best take a good look
What should school really provide
A text and desk
Or should they all get equal rights
to you I do ask
What does school really mean
Deep inside my heart
A place for our future world
To get a great head start

# Beginning of the End

I have recently discovered an ancient
Old myth of life
And no it is not, that I can't live
Without a wife
It has to do with the fuel you use
To light your fire
They say you push yourself
To a place that is higher
It has to do with the way you burn the fuel
That you ingest
You can take the road of mediocrity
Or you can be the best
It has to with the place you
Choose to carry out
This should be the joy of your life
Without a single doubt
It has to do with the nest
Upon which you were hatched
Can you please yourself first
Or are you too attached
I have discovered that living for me
Can never have an end

You all are such a joy here in class
There is nothing we can't do
Never do I have a fear of trying
Something new
Let's stop what we are doing and head
Out for a walk in the sun
Learning about the Poppy's, singing
And having fun
It is a joy to see you all accepting
Everyone for who they are
This will allow you all, in life,
To make it very far
I look out at you sitting there
Giving thought to what you write
Not just throwing words down on paper
But really using your insight
Thank you from the bottom of my heart
For another wonderful day
I really do not like the fact that
One day you will go away

# Someone

If I only had someone to share with me
The sound of a crashing wave
As love for life grows inside of my soul
Each and every day
Someone to share a smile with
That does not have to go away
Someone to shed a tear with
On one of those bad days
Someone to raise a child with
Give them love and tender care
Someone to confide all your dreams in
A person that is rare
Someone that is beautiful both on the inside
And the out
The inner beauty within, the most important
Without the slightest doubt
Soon that someone will appear
Drop down from heaven above
For she will be a fortunate woman
Acquiring all of my love

# The Class of 2000

Good evening ladies and gentlemen
Boys and girls, moms and dads
I am sure you will be amazed as you
Watch your lasses and lads
For more than eight months now
I have had the privilege to get to know
Each student as an individual
Yet watch how easily they flew
They have made my first year teaching
An event that filled my heart
The end is coming near and I regret
We have to part
Each and every one of you has touched
My life in every way
This poem is a gift to you
An attempt to simply repay
I ponder long with how to start
Amber's name did appear
Our favorite Ninja Turtle
I am you moved up here

My walks into class with a smile
That lasts forever
Then Penny walks by, right behind her
Two whispers by whatever
These two girls have a friendship that
Will last a day or so
I have watched it grow together
Like two boys I once did know
When I look at these young men
I see a star shining bright
No matter how hard task at hand
Buck will always give a fight
Cody is a pleasure to have in class
He is as polite as can be
I call him the candy man
He always shares with me
If this young lady could just ride a horse
I am afraid, that's all she'd do
Thank God school interests Gabe
Or I would never have gotten to know you

Haley comes to play with us
Most every afternoon
I wish she could just stay thru
The month of June
Haley also joined our class midway
Thru this year
Her pretty little smile
Most any disease it will cure
This young man can do it all
Play the piano like the wind
Isaiah, you are a wonderful student
And a true to heart friend
We have known each other for
A lifetime it seems
Each day you are in class is a pleasure for me
Jamie seems
If there ever was a student who
Gave it her all
Jamie R. will work her little heart
Out instead of taking a fall

Jason, you are a whiz kid
Math seems to be your forte
I look forward to working with you
Each and every day
Jed can wear a smile over
The simplest thing
A bright spot in each day this
Young man does bring
Every morning I get the scoop
The latest update
On a scale of 1 to 10
Jennifer does highly rate
He has a sense of humor and a
Mind of great content
Every Time I need his knowledge
J.D. does always lent
This young lady is a total package
From dancing to straight as
Katherine has a very bright future
Ahead in her days

When it comes to feelings and emotions
Kristian shows them all
Never is she afraid to stand up to
Take a fall
Everything that Leah does is as smooth
As new fallen snow
From math to swimming, dance to sparks
She has a steady flow
I have never known someone who could
Be so loud and yet so shy
Lego you make each rainy day a

Beautiful bright blue sky
She is the hug queen
She seems to go out of her way
Mattie knows when you're down and
Can cheer up the worst of days
Melanie always makes me cards
Just to say hello
It may be as simple as a plain piece of paper
But I love it you know

This young lady has heart that is
As big as the sun
No matter what you choose to do
Melissa, you will be number one
Micha is not afraid to speak his mind
And rightfully so
This life has a lot in store for you
Ahead you will always go
Every day when I call roll
Hey, is Nadia here yet
She may be late but her work is always
Done on that you can bet
When you think about a student that
Can do most anything

Inside your head, the name Ryan D
Should let out a ring
He is the most thoughtful young man
He cares about his friend
Ryan Freeman will come out on top
In the very end

Shaun is a gentleman always lending
A helping hand
I am glad you get to join our already
Wonderful band
Last but not least, is Travis
Whose heart does go out
He loves his friends and family all
Without a doubt

# Best of the Best

Seventeen years ago, I sat where you are
As student in the 5th grade
Sherri taught me what it is like not
To be afraid
That many years later, our lives did
Rejoin again
This time she is my mentor and
A wonderful friend
You are all very lucky to be taught
By Mrs. Potter
There is not a better place, parents
For your son and daughter
She can give and give and never
Expect it to be repaid
A lasting impression on whatever
She has touched is definitely made
All her colleagues feel the same
You should not be surprised to hear
They have voted Mrs. Potter
Redwood Teacher of the Year
I only hear one question
What took you so long
To reward such a gatekeeper
Of what is right or wrong
Thank you Sherri for being my teacher
Both in the beginning and the end
But thank you most Mrs. Potter for
Just being my friend

# Worthwhile

Does hard work really payoff or
Is that a long told myth
Is commitment the source of success
That all who <u>do</u>, start with
Can determination take you places
That once was a blink of an eye
If one had all the desire in the world
Is the limit really the sky
Or is it maturation, the key
To open up the door
Could dedication be the way to
Experience that one step more
An open mind must be a part of your
Way to feel a dream
An open heart to the table you must
Centrally always bring
Take all these natural ingredients and
Serve them up with a smile
The choices you have made for your life
Suddenly become worthwhile

# Two Way Street

To actually compare oneself to
Another is not exactly fair
What is important to you
The other may really not care
Some may feel what they do is so grand
All must see just that
Not everyone wears the exactly the same size
And color of hat
The freedom of choice should be just that
Not prison as a consequence
Respect should be earned
Not just given for dollars and cents
If you are not accepted because of a
Predetermined event
Maybe your assailant should look around
For another hint
That in the game of tug of war
These are two ways to win
You end up with all the rope
But you will not be standing in the end
You can count on waking up from a
Dream-filled sleepy night

You can tell the difference between
What is wrong or right
You can count on friends and family
Always being there for you
You can count on the sun eventually
Shining through
You can count on the birds to sing their song
Every new Spring
You can count on the groom to give
His bride a ring
You can count on the night to come
Just like the day
You can count on life and death
In some mysterious way
But most of all, you can count on
God to work his wonderful power
For He is on my side during this
Trying hour
But all good things must come to an end
A lesson in life to learn
Unfortunately, the day has come for
Us to take our turn

# So Long

What a year we have had together
This group of 31
We have basically redefined that ancient
old word called fun
We have taught each other "life" and
What it is to "love
We have learned that all good things
Do eventually rise above
We have been to many places
Yontucket being the best
That's not to say we did not
Enjoy all the rest
So wipe the tears from your eyes and
Hold your chin up tall
Because I can say from the bottom of
My heart, I truly love you all

# Finally Over

There are many moments in our lives that
Make it all worthwhile
Today was one of those special days
In which to really smile
A message was delivered to me
Great news it did share
For I have crossed over that bridge
That was seemingly unfair
Now that I have made it past
This test of knowledge and wit
I will see to it that you do not have to go
Thru it
For teaching is a way of like
In which you choose to live
No exam you should weigh so much
For this life you want to live
That is all behind me
My future bright and fair
I am a teacher now
With all I will share

# Mask

A mask is paint a clown put on
To be someone they're not
Such happy people they are
Or at least that's what we thought
A uniform is what a soldier wears
To show their pride in self
Yet the body underneath can be
Frail as an old shelf
A title is a group of words an author
Gives their book
Should you judge it by its cover
Or should you take a good long look
A label is a name given those groups
Certain thinking together
Is it fair to place one there
Or should you look even further
Because there's rust covering a car
Does not mean its junk
Before you judge an individual
Let them show you their trunk
We all love to be clowns and
Wear these masks of doubt
But it's who we are inside our souls
That really does make it count

# Morgan

On a glorious day in September
A breath of fresh air appeared on earth
The most beautiful event that God has created
That of giving birth
A twinkle in your eyes appear
Without a hesitation
Endless love, you give this child
Without any reservation
Her beauty is that of an angel
Her skin as soft as snow
Thank you for making us a part
Allowing us to watch her grow
If there ever was the thought
Can we do this task
The answer is self-evident
no more need to ask
For Morgan is so fortunate to have been born
On that day
To such wonderful people for you
We always pray

Mrs. Daniel

You always help us with our projects
Our reading and our homework
You come enough to keep us going
Especially when we lag
You are there for us when we are happy
Or when we're sad
You are kind of like our mommy's
And makes us feel real glad

# Christmas

This is the time of year my spirit
Comes alive
The giving and receiving of love, my heart
It does drive
Knowing I have a family to share my existence
With each day
Especially in this glorious season of
Happiness in a righteous way
Christmas is so special
The joy it brings to earth
Mary, Joseph, the 3 wise men and
Jesus Christ's birth
Let's teach mankind the true meaning of
This time of year
Then celebrate with those you love
A season full of cheer

# Participating

The question is being asked today
if Christina will join in
No matter the answer, being here,
For myself, I win
To the answer, the questions about
Why I am ill
Is beneath this flesh that has
A strong will
Today has been a challenge
Art I did not know
But exciting and expressive with
Writing I will grow
I pray that she opens her heart to
The voice and the ask
To the challenge and opportunity
To reveal her mask
We started off strong, adversity
Came on fast
True Love is real and should always last
My intention today is to accept the things
I cannot change
And allow her the opportunity to take whatever is
necessary to rearrange
For now I will slow down and wait for her
Answer she gave
And accept my actions and be strong and brave

# Frustrated

What happened to the structure your website says
So come here
Yet each day goes by, some still live in fear
Last weekend shouldn't have happened
People are mad
As a compassionate man, that really makes me sad
I listen, observe and watch with my heart
As one of us unfortunately soon has to part
The leader needs to see what is happening here
The love, the pain, the sweet, the tear
Each moment that goes by and issues aren't addressed
The pain grows deeper and no one gets rest
We all came to LHC seeking a new way of life
Mine has to rekindle with my amazing wife
Let's all refocus our mission and goal
To leave this spiritual place new and whole
You all are amazing in your own special way
May you sleep well tonight to a new beautiful day

# True Love

When you know it, you know it
There is no doubt
From the highest mountain top
You just want to shout
Your heart fills with joy
that makes you flutter like a bee
For everyone in the world to
Stop, stare and see
The amazing feeling you share
From within your soul
How much joy and happiness
That makes you whole
For true love only comes once in
My life
I will truly guard it with
Will you be my wife
Her beauty is magnificent
I tell her every day
I will meet her in Sante Fe
I will never stop loving her

As long as I am alive
She gives me honesty and hope
I will forever to thrive
Quit, I will not, for I do not know how
But never or she, he's asked,
So I will for now
True love lasts forever and she is the one
I will prove to her my promise
Before I am done
I took the vows before God
And said I do
Tina Marie, I will always love you

# Liar

When you give someone advice and
It is not asked for
Be sure you do remember when you're
Called out on the floor
It could be really embarrassing for
All that is in the room
The tension could increase the mood
Turns it into gloom
It doesn't need to happen
If you would just remember what you said
Instead of being accused and
Losing you head
The truth does prevail
It certainly does come out
There were others in the room
When you said it without a doubt
Next time you say I don't remember
Saying I gave you advice
Before you open your mouth
Maybe you should think twice

# Tourettes

Hey Darin and Marcy I finally found out, I have Tourettes Holly Shit!

"You can them all little Son of A Bitches and get away with it!"

In Tau Kappa Epsilon my Fraternal name was "Twitch"

A Term of Endearment, a nickname I will never ditch

Living 35 years of my life always wondering why

I would go from complete laughter to a sudden tearful cry

Teased my entire childhood, mainly by those we "trust"

Adults were the worst of all; High School was a Fucking bust

Called a Son of A Bitch by Dale Thomas and literally kicked out of class

And Jeff Nynehouse, "I can't handle you on the bus" what a Fucking Ass

My label given to me has long been mislead

Even those who have this "Gift" have been mislead

Medication was prescribed, what a fiasco that became

It is not okay for medical professionals to cause "US" to go insane

The only neurological disorder known to those prescribing drugs

Sorry Dr Narus, LOVE is the answers; please start prescribing "Hugs"

"I want some of what you're on, can I have some "SHIT"

"I have Tourettes, you want some of "IT"

My final straw came when I was arrested and thrown in jail

"DUI other than Alcohol", just try and make bail

Before you judge those of us who suffer from this pain

Think to yourself, what do I have to gain?

We all have a disability; just take a look in the mirror

"Can I walk on water", or do I just have a fear

How to accept others, no matter the Twitch, The Glasses or The Creed

Thank God for those who can understand why I choose to smoke weed

It is the only true relief I have ever had other than LOVE

"Footprints In The Sand" my friends, Thank You God above

So often people walk away or simply want to ignore

Maybe Tourettes will go away, we won't have to deal with

"THEM" anymore

To all of you that have this "Gift", the one that makes me,

ME

Don't ever let them put you the "Box", live and be free

I am proud of my life each and every day

Of course there are times I think, "Make IT go away"

So when you are passing judgement or "Choosing" to

discriminate

You are one of "THEM", you are causing the HATE!!!


Billy Hartwick
Woodland Villa, Klamath, California
7/22/2019
The Beginning!
Born Feb. 8$^{th}$ 1965